PRIMARY SOURCE DETECTIVES

WHO MARCHED FOR CIVIL RIGHTS?

Richard Spilsbury

Heinemann
LIBRARY

Chicago, Illinois

Edited by Andrew Farrow, Patrick Catel, and Vaarunika Dharmapala
Designed by Steve Mead
Original illustrations © Capstone Global Library Ltd 2014
Illustrated by HL Studios
Picture research by Ruth Blair
Originated by Capstone Global Library Ltd
Printed in China

17 16 15 14 13
10 9 8 7 6 5 4 3 2 1

Library of Congress Cataloging-in-Publication Data

Spilsbury, Richard, 1963-
  Who marched for civil rights? / Richard Spilsbury.
      pages cm.—(Primary source detectives)
  Includes bibliographical references and index.
  ISBN 978-1-4329-9604-8 (hb)—ISBN 978-1-4329-9611-6 (pb) 1. African Americans—Civil rights—History—20th century—Juvenile literature. 2. Civil rights workers—United States—History—20th century—Juvenile literature. 3. Civil rights movements—United States—History—20th century—Juvenile literature. 4. United States—Race relations—Juvenile literature. I. Title.

  E185.61.S74 2014
  323.1196'0730904—dc23
  2013015846

Acknowledgments
We would like to thank the following for permission to reproduce photographs: Alamy pp. 47 (© Everett Collection Historical), 56 (© Frances Roberts); BCRI Oral History Project, Birmingham Civil Rights Institute, Alabama p. 51; Corbis pp. 12 & 40 (© Bettmann), 55 (© Jeff Haller/Keyhole Photo); Getty Images pp. 5 (AFP), 8 (Ed Clark/Time Life Pictures), 18 (Mario Tama), 21 (Patrick A. Burns/New York Times Co.), 28 (Michael Ochs Archives), 31 (Popperfoto), 32 (PhotoQuest), 38 (AFP), 42 (William Lovelace/Express), 45 (Redferns), 49 (Rolls Press/Popperfoto), 53; Library of Congress p. 17 (web site screengrab); Shutterstock p. 23 (© SeanPavonePhoto); pp. 15 & 24 sourced from The Martin Luther King, Jr. Papers Project, Stanford University; Topfoto pp. 10 (AP), 27 (Topham/AP), 33 (The Granger Collection).

Cover photograph of Martin Luther King, Jr., reproduced with permission of Getty Images (Hulton Archive).

Permission to reproduce the transcribed interview on page 51 was kindly granted by BCRI Oral History Project, Birmingham Civil Rights Institute, Birmingham, Alabama.

Every effort has been made to contact copyright holders of material reproduced in this book. Any omissions will be rectified in subsequent printings if notice is given to the publisher.

CONTENTS

WASHINGTON '63 4

WHAT WERE CIVIL RIGHTS? 6

WHY DID PEOPLE MARCH FOR CIVIL RIGHTS? 12

WHAT KIND OF PEOPLE WERE THEY? 18

WHERE DID PEOPLE MARCH? 26

WHAT HAPPENED TO PEOPLE
ON THE MARCHES? 36

WHAT HAPPENED TO MARCHERS
AFTERWARD?...48

WHY WERE THE MARCHES SIGNIFICANT? 52

TIMELINE 58

GLOSSARY..60

FIND OUT MORE 62

INDEX...64

Some words are shown in bold, **like this**. You can find out what they mean by looking in the glossary.

WASHINGTON '63

*Washington, Aug. 28: More than 200,000 Americans, most of them black but many of them white, demonstrated here today for a full and speedy program of **civil rights** and equal job opportunities...This vast throng proclaimed in march and song and through the speeches of their leaders that they were still waiting for [better civil rights] and the jobs... But if the crowd was good-natured, the underlying tone was one of dead seriousness. The emphasis was on "freedom" and "now."*

E. W. Kenworthy, *New York Times*

Newspaper reports about the 1963 March on Washington for Jobs and Freedom appeared in newspapers across the United States and overseas. Most people agreed the march had been a success. Twice the expected number of protestors had marched demanding **equality** for black people, and the event had been peaceful.

RELIEF

Behind the scenes, organizers were breathing a sigh of relief. There had been a lot of opposition to the march. President John F. Kennedy was worried it would encourage government opposition to changing civil rights laws by sparking violence between marchers and groups opposing the march. These included political groups such as the **Ku Klux Klan (KKK)** who did not want equality for black people.

Organizers were also worried about the speeches. For example, John Lewis, the leader of a civil rights organization called the **Student Nonviolent Coordinating Committee (SNCC)**, had planned to say, "We will...take matters into our own hands and create a source of power... that...would assure us a victory." But organizers had persuaded him in the hours before speaking to change the words. The worry was that some people might think it was a call to be violent, and that such a message risked losing popular support for the movement. Instead, he said: "For those who have said, 'Be patient and wait!' we must say...we do not want to be free gradually, we want our freedom, and we want it now."

▲ Martin Luther King, Jr., waves to a massive crowd of civil rights marchers from the steps of the Lincoln Memorial in Washington, D.C.

Lewis's powerful message succeeded in showing support for people pushing for urgent civil rights changes without encouraging violence. However, the last speech, by civil rights leader Martin Luther King, Jr., had the biggest impact on the crowd, reporters, and TV audiences. He spoke from his heart and not from his script, saying: "I have a dream that my four little children will one day live in a nation where they will not be judged by the color of their skin but by the content of their character."

King's powerful, calm words showed that he believed the quest for equality was just, and although it might take time, it would succeed. His speech went on to become one of the most famous in U.S. history. This march was the first time that the message of a U.S. civil rights protest had reached a widespread audience. But why had people decided they had to march? What kind of people were they, and where did they march?

WHAT WERE CIVIL RIGHTS?

Little Rock was separated...there were the white ladies bathroom and the black ladies' bathroom... One day, I...decided that I wanted to know what was in a white ladies' bathroom that I couldn't see...so I went in there and, here are all these cops banging on the door... My mother was screaming, "Don't kill her!"... And there was nothing but toilets in there.

Melba Pattillo

Melba Pattillo was a teenager in the town of Little Rock, Arkansas, in the 1950s. The quote above is from an interview in later life describing what she experienced as a girl. Melba was just one of millions of U.S. citizens who could not choose where to go to the bathroom, eat, study, or sit on a bus because she was black.

The U.S. Constitution said all Americans were equal citizens. But a famous court case called Plessy v. Ferguson in 1896 established the idea that states could insist on "separate but equal" treatment for citizens based on their skin color or race. Many black people in the United States lived in the South in states such as Arkansas. Following the court case, every southern state had created **Jim Crow laws**. These made it law for black citizens to have separate, poorer public facilities and work opportunities and fewer chances to improve their status than white people. This was racial **segregation**.

CIVIL RIGHTS MOVEMENT

Most people believe that everyone should have the right to say what they think, vote for the leaders they want, receive equal protection from the law, and not face **discrimination**. These are civil rights. There have been struggles in many countries to improve the civil rights of different groups of people, but the **civil rights movement** usually refers to the decade or so from the mid-1950s when black Americans struggled to gain key civil rights.

This was a difficult and often violent struggle for the people involved. Here is what happened when Melba Pattillo tried to enroll at the whites-only Central High School in Little Rock:

> There [was] a mob in front of the school...filled with layers...
> of red-faced angry people... jeering... [Then] I saw all these
> faces looking at me...what they're turning around for is to kill you...
> I back up in astonishment...and my mother just screamed at me, she
> said, "I tell you, get to the car now! Listen to me, leave me if you
> have to, get to the car!"... We both got in the car...and we [escaped
> from the] mob.

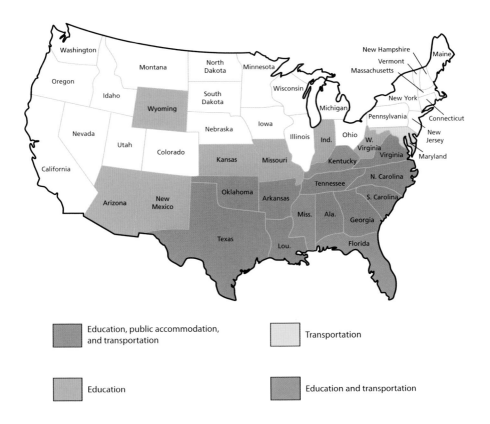

▲ From the late 19th century to the mid-20th century in the United States, Jim Crow laws of various sorts were official in most southern and eastern states. This map shows what categories of Jim Crow laws applied in each state.

GRADUAL CHANGE

In the 1950s, there was growing frustration among black Americans about segregation. Some had recently returned home from World War II (1939–1945), where they had fought in the same forces as white soldiers against the same enemies. Many felt that Nazi **persecution** and segregation of Jewish people was similar to the treatment of black people in the United States. In some states, Jim Crow laws were gradually changing. This was partly through the increasing role of the **National Association for the Advancement of Colored People (NAACP)**. The group's founders included W. E. B. DuBois, the first black person to gain a doctorate (a high-level degree) from Harvard University, and Mary White Ovington, a white woman whose grandparents had worked to end slavery in the 19th century. NAACP members gave financial and legal support to help black people fight court cases to, for example, gain equal educational opportunities.

DOLL TEST

Psychologists Kenneth and Mamie Clark presented the results of their "doll test" as evidence at Brown v. Board of Education. Black children were shown four plastic dolls, identical except for the color of their "skin." They said they preferred to play with the white doll and attributed more positive characteristics to it than the black one. Doctors concluded that "prejudice, discrimination, and segregation" caused black children to develop a sense of inferiority and self-hatred.

▼ NAACP lawyer Thurgood Marshall (see page 9) speaks to reporters.

BROWN V. BOARD OF EDUCATION

In 1954, the lead NAACP lawyer, Thurgood Marshall, and his team won a very important legal case called **Brown v. Board of Education**. They presented evidence to the U.S. **Supreme Court** from five state court cases in which black people had been unsuccessful at ending school segregation. This included photos of poor conditions in black schools and psychologists' reports proving how segregation harmed black children.

The Supreme Court concluded that all segregation of public schools was illegal. This was a significant step in improving civil rights for black Americans, but there was great resistance to changing Jim Crow school segregation laws in the South. A student named James A. Banks recalls: "The white school boards controlled both black and white schools. Consequently, for black teachers to spread the word about the [Brown v. Board] decision, especially among students, would probably have been considered a subversive and dangerous act."

HISTORY DETECTIVES:
WHAT IS RESEARCH?

Historical research starts with one or more questions or problems we want to resolve. Research can be very time-consuming, so how do you start and keep on track?

One way is by using a KWL chart. This is a graphic organizer with three columns headed "what I know," "what I want to know," and "what I have learned." The first column is your chance to say what you already know or think you know about the topic. Use the second column to help you focus on what is required in your research. Your research results can go in the last column.

TAKING ACTION

Most schools in the South remained segregated after Brown v. Board of Education, because forcing change through legal cases was slow. From the mid-1950s onward, more and more civil rights protestors took **direct action** to try to speed up change. Direct action is when people carry out public acts that disrupt or break the law in order to raise awareness of an issue. Rosa Parks's refusal to give up her seat to a white woman on a public bus in Montgomery, Alabama, in 1955 was an early example. The NAACP planned this action and used Parks's arrest to spark a **boycott** of city buses. After 13 months of lost business and bad publicity, the state made segregation illegal on its buses.

Other famous examples of taking action for civil rights include the Little Rock Nine. Nine black children, including Melba Pattillo (see pages 6 and 7), tried to attend a white-only school in 1957. The resulting violence and protests against segregation led to the U.S. government stepping in to force the governor of Arkansas, Orval Faubus, to **desegregate** its schools. Watch an interview with Governor Faubus in which he explains why he prevented the Little Rock Nine from going to school: www.hrc.utexas.edu/multimedia/video/2008/wallace/faubus_orval.html.

▼ Fifteen-year-old Elizabeth Eckford (in sunglasses) walks past angry white students during the Little Rock Nine action.

ORVAL FAUBUS
1910–1994

BORN: Combs, Arkansas

ROLE: Governor of Arkansas from 1954 to 1967. In 1957, he ordered the **National Guard** to stop black children from going to Little Rock High School to keep law and order. President Dwight D. Eisenhower ordered government troops in to protect the Little Rock Nine so that they could attend school.

Did You Know?

Faubus ended segregation in Arkansas on state public transportation when he was first elected governor.

DANGER

It is difficult to imagine now how strongly some white people felt about civil rights campaigners in the 1950s. Many of these people were members of groups such as the Ku Klux Klan (KKK). The KKK was a terrorist organization that pursued actions included **firebombing** homes and churches and **lynching**. Lynching involved a mob seizing, beating, and usually violently killing people. In 1957, for example, the KKK offered a $10,000 reward to anyone who killed one of the Little Rock Nine.

HISTORY DETECTIVES: SOURCES

Diaries, interviews, autobiographies, and photos are primary sources, or records of events created at the time being studied. Secondary sources are interpretations and analyses of primary sources. They are usually created by people who were not there at the time. Examples include books, biographies, and movies. Secondary sources can provide good overviews to direct research, but a range of primary sources can add details and bring the past to life.

WHY DID PEOPLE MARCH FOR CIVIL RIGHTS?

From winter 1961, civil rights protestors in Albany, Georgia, ran a campaign to end segregation on buses. Hundreds of volunteers (many of whom were students) met in churches. They marched to and occupied the bus station. They recited prayers and sang songs together, refusing to be moved on by police. One protestor, Bernice Johnson Reagon, recalls how it felt:

> *For many people like me, the highest point of our lives was when we gathered in those mass meetings, and when we marched... We were bonded to each other, not because we went to school together, or were in the same social club. Not because we worked on the same job, but because we had decided that we would put everything on the line to fight racism in our community.*

▼ These Albany marchers kneel and pray before being arrested for marching in 1961.

Protestors expected a violent response from Albany police, but instead they were peacefully arrested. The campaign—called the Albany Movement—continued for many months. More than 1,000 people were arrested and taken to jails outside the county, to prevent further protests around Albany's jails. Many people describe Albany as a failure in the civil rights movement because it did not end with desegregation, and because organizers had to spend a lot of money getting protestors out of jail. Yet this was the first time that a large civil rights march had taken place, and it made it clear to organizers that mass protests could have a big impact.

HISTORY DETECTIVES: A BALANCED VIEW

Primary sources about the same events can express very different opinions. In the examples below, two newspaper editorials describe the same march in Albany. However, one reports that it was a nuisance for the locals, while the other says it was a nuisance that the civil rights movement had to go through another unnecessary struggle. In your research, it is very useful to show both sides, because it can highlight different feelings about the same moments in history.

Editorial:
Albany Bears Up Well
Our sympathy goes out to the people of Albany, over their difficulty. The patient restraint they have exhibited, the good judgment shown by their officials and especially the manner in which Albany's chief of police has enforced the law and maintained order has won the admiration of countless thousands.
The Birmingham Post-Herald
August 4, 1962

Editorial:
Another Round in a Wasteful Fight
The latest racial incident in Albany, Georgia, is depressing, not because of violence, for there was none, but because it is but another dreary round in a fight so wasteful of human energy. The eventual outcome of the struggle is no longer in doubt. Segregation is doomed, and even the extreme **segregationists** know they are only engaged in a holding action.
The Louisville Courier Journal
July 16, 1962

MARCHES AND OTHER PROTESTS

Marches are obvious ways to show unity for a common cause. They often start or end with speeches, and marchers may chant slogans, sing songs, and carry signs with messages as they walk. These help attract attention and spread the marchers' message to the public wherever they pass, unlike a meeting that happens in one place. Since marches are public, they also attract interest from the media, which can spread the message even further.

Marching was just one of the types of group direct action protest used by civil rights protestors. For example, in February 1960, four black students from North Carolina Agriculture and Technical College sat down in the white-only lunch counter at the Woolworth's store in Greensboro, North Carolina. They were refused service, but they remained sitting until closing time. The next morning, they were joined by 20 more students, and the day after that by 63 more. After five days, there were 300 protestors. After some students were arrested, **sit-in** protests spread to segregated lunch counters at many Woolworth's. After six months of sit-ins, sales had dropped by a third, forcing Woolworth's to end segregation.

FREEDOM RIDES

The **freedom rides** of May 1961 were another group direct action protest, this time against segregation on buses and in stations. Thirteen people—blacks and whites—boarded and sat together on two buses that set off from Washington, D.C., to stop off at towns and cities in the South. One bus was firebombed in Alabama, and riders were badly beaten with pipes and chains by white people furious at what they were doing. Some riders were arrested or hospitalized, but more riders joined the route. Images and reports of burning buses and beaten riders gained national attention.

One freedom rider, Hank Thomas, explained in an interview later how the riders expected trouble and why they made a point of being well-dressed:

[We were] well-dressed, mannerly, orderly black folks just asking for what ordinary Americans were asking for. And the contrast between us and the mob was these white toughs who spoke poor English and everything about them seemed to say these are uneducated folks... and we're the ones that are being refused service... We wanted that contrast to be there.

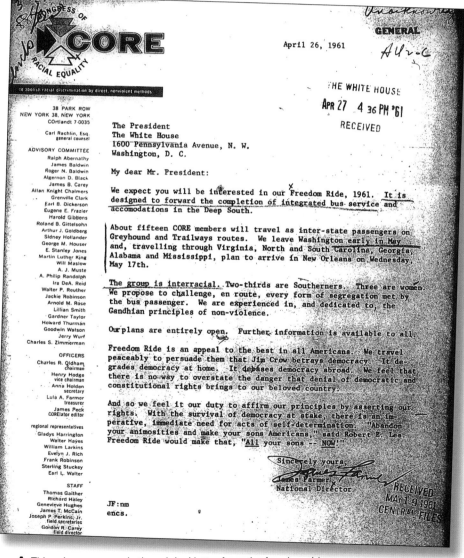

▲ This primary source is the original letter from the freedom riders to the president to announce their intention to confront segregation in the South.

AVOIDING VIOLENCE

One of the most important principles of the civil rights protests was that they should be nonviolent. This meant that even if marchers were pushed, hit, spat at, or otherwise provoked, they should never fight back. Mohandas Gandhi was a great influence on some civil rights leaders such as Martin Luther King, Jr. Gandhi had used nonviolent protest against British rule to gain eventual independence for India. King was an increasingly important civil rights leader and therefore a target for violence from segregationists. However, during the boycotts, he chose not to have armed bodyguards for protection, but instead to face arrest and physical violence. He even reacted with compassion when extremists firebombed his home. King developed several key beliefs about nonviolence:

- Nonviolence aims to gain understanding of your enemy.
- You should expect to suffer for your cause.
- Nonviolence is both in action and in thought.

WHO IN HISTORY

MOHANDAS GANDHI
1869–1948
BORN: Porbandar, India

ROLE: Gandhi developed and popularized mass nonviolent protest against British rulers in South Africa and India. For example, when Great Britain put a tax on salt, Gandhi walked over 200 miles (320 kilometers) to the sea to make his own salt, which was illegal. Thousands of Indians joined him in his march, and many were arrested and treated badly, but they did not fight back. Gandhi led many nonviolent protests like this, and they influenced protest movements worldwide.

Did You Know?

Even though he was famous and wealthy, Gandhi spun his own cotton cloth to make his clothing.

King was a **Baptist** church leader in Montgomery, Alabama, and talked about nonviolent protests to his **congregation**. He joined with other black religious leaders and civil rights protestors to form the **Southern Christian Leadership Conference (SCLC)**, which encouraged the use of nonviolence in the South. King said:

> *Nonviolence is a powerful and just weapon which cuts without wounding and ennobles the man who wields it. It is a sword that heals.*

◀ Web sites such as the Library of Congress Voices of Civil Rights pages provide invaluable collections of primary sources.

OTHER WAYS

Some civil rights marchers struggled with the idea that nonviolence was the only way to protest, especially after witnessing or experiencing violence themselves. Rob Williams was an NAACP leader who lived in Monroe, North Carolina, where there was widespread persecution by the KKK of any black people trying to fight for civil rights. He grew frustrated by this and how white courts in the state did not give fair trials or protection to black people. Williams formed an armed group called the Black Guard, which was committed to the protection of Monroe's black population. In 1959, he said:

> *It is time for [black] men to stand up and be men and if it is necessary for us to die we must be willing to die. If it is necessary for us to kill we must be willing to kill.*

Malcolm X and those involved in the black power movement (see pages 48–49) also questioned nonviolence in the early 1960s.

WHAT KIND OF PEOPLE WERE THEY?

In summer 2008, filmmaker Robin Fryday went to Alabama to research a documentary about participants in civil rights marches and other protesters who were still living. She met many people who had taken part in marches. But one interviewee in Birmingham asked if she had met the barber. Fryday went to the shop she was directed to. She said: "It's a tiny little barber shop, but every inch of space was covered with photographs and newspaper clippings and memorabilia from the civil rights movement... The shop was almost like a living museum."

James Armstrong had been a barber in the city for 50 years after returning from fighting in World War II. He had carried a flag in a famous Selma-to-Montgomery march in 1965 (see pages 36–39). He had battled segregation in different ways, such as by getting his children into an all-white school and buying a home in a white neighborhood.

◀ James Armstrong's barber shop was one of several focal points for civil rights discussions in the segregated city of Birmingham, Alabama, during the 1950s and 1960s.

Over the years, Armstrong had talked and debated with thousands of customers about civil rights and encouraged them to get involved in civil rights protests. He said: "If you want a voice, you have to vote; you can't complain about nothing if you don't vote… Dying isn't the worst thing a man can do. The worst thing a man can do is nothing."

Fryday used interviews with Armstrong as a central thread through her film, which went on to get an Oscar nomination. She said about him: "James Armstrong was so ordinary yet so extraordinary. As [Armstrong] says in the film, he wanted to live with a purpose, and I carry those words with me." Discover more about the film that Robin Fryday made at barberofbirmingham.com.

RANGE

Civil rights marchers came from all walks of life. For example, William Lewis Moore was a postal worker, Jackie Robinson was a famous retired baseball player, Fannie Hamer worked in cotton fields, Frederick Walbert was a music teacher, and Viola Liuzzo was a housewife. Most marchers were black, but some were white. Some were old, while others were young. Sheyann Webb was just eight years old when she was inspired to march at Selma, Alabama, in 1965, after hearing King talk at a church meeting. She felt very strongly about marching, but she was so scared that she wrote plans for her own funeral just in case!

HISTORY DETECTIVES: ORAL HISTORY

Have you ever listened to older people recalling when they were young? This is known as oral history. Some historians make recordings of oral history to capture such memories. When you are researching recent historical events, see if you can interview someone who was there. Plan what questions you want to ask. For example, don't ask about pets or hobbies if you are trying to find out more about protests. Remember to record in a place without background noise so that it does not ruin the recording.

STUDENTS

Diane Nash grew up in Chicago, Illinois, where there was no official segregation. But when she went to college in Nashville, Tennessee, in the late 1950s, she was shocked not only to experience segregation, but also by the lack of interest on the campus about improving civil rights. She said:

> I recall talking to a number of people in the dormitories at school and on campus, and asking them if they knew any people who were trying …to bring about some type of change. And I remember…getting almost depressed, because I encountered what I thought was so much apathy.

But colleges were a major focus for the civil rights movement. From the mid-1950s onward, more colleges in the South were starting to desegregate. More white students met and spent time with black students on campus than before, and they grew angry about injustices in their country, including the infamous case of Emmett Till (see below). Students were becoming more interested in free speech and not automatically conforming to what society expected of them.

WHO IN HISTORY

EMMETT TILL
1941–1955
BORN: Chicago, Illinois

ROLE: Emmett Till was a 14-year-old black boy visiting relatives in Mississippi. He made the fatal mistake of flirting with a white woman, and he was then lynched. His body was thrown in a river. A court found the men who admitted to kidnapping him not guilty. The men later admitted to killing Till. Till's death and photos of his beaten body made many people in northern cities realize the harshness of life for black people in the South.

Did You Know?

Emmett loved jokes so much that he paid people to tell them to him.

Some students became motivated to march after experiencing racism in the South. Others, such as John Lewis, grew up in the South. He was the son of poor black farmers in Alabama, so he knew about segregation firsthand. He was arrested and beaten many times as a freedom rider and went on to help coordinate marches across the United States. The students who became marchers were not just at southern universities. Bob Moses grew up in New York and studied at Harvard University. He and other northern students traveled to the South to try to encourage black people there to register to vote.

CANCELED MARCH

Bayard Rustin was a student and teacher who was a major figure in the civil rights marches. In 1941, with A. Philip Randolph, he planned a march in Washington, D.C., to end segregation in arms (weapon) factories. These factories were booming during World War II, but only white people could get jobs there. They called the march off after meeting President Franklin D. Roosevelt, who changed laws to make it easier for black people to work in the factories. Randolph later organized the 1963 march (see pages 4–5 and 32–33).

▲ This shows civil rights leader Bayard Rustin.

CHURCH COMMUNITY

The Baptist Church in the South was more than a place for black people to worship; it was also a center of their community. The church helped people sort out disputes, financial problems, gave support to those in need, and was a place where marches were publicized. Many people became marchers after hearing speeches and singing songs in church.

Martin Luther King, Jr., Fred Shuttlesworth, and Ralph Abernathy are among the most famous Baptist leaders who marched. King joined the movement after encouragement from organizers of the Montgomery Bus Boycotts. They knew that if King joined the boycott, then so might many members of his congregation. People in the civil rights movement knew that Baptist churches in the South were a safe haven for black people. In church, black people might be persuaded to have the courage to take direct action. Getting the support of congregations could also raise funds for the cause.

People from other faiths also marched. Abraham Joshua Heschel was a Jewish rabbi who was expelled from Germany during World War II and eventually settled in the United States. He walked arm-in-arm with King at the famous Selma–Montgomery marches (see pages 36–39). Heschel believed that marching was a religious activity—not only in showing compassion for the oppressed, but also as a focus of prayer. He said:

For many of us the march from Selma to Montgomery was about protest and prayer. Legs are not lips and walking is not kneeling. And yet our legs uttered songs. Even without words, our march was worship. I felt my legs were praying.

UNREST IN THE CHURCH

Religious protestors, like any others, faced hostilities from the white community and the Ku Klux Klan for supporting civil rights protests. But some also faced disapproval from their religious leaders. In 1963, Father Maurice Ouellet wrote to Catholic leader Archbishop Toolen to ask official permission for Ouellet and other members of his Catholic **mission** to participate in marches. Toolen was concerned that the association with unrest and violence would drive away worshippers from the church.

In response to Ouellet's request, Toolen wrote:

> I won't stand for any priest...going in parades or sit-ins... The marches...have done absolutely no good... Of course, you realize you are stirring up great trouble for yourself, as I have told you, Selma and the surrounding country as far as [black people are] concerned is and always has been the worst in the state. They hate [black people], and hate [them] worse than they love the Church.

Ouellet did not march, but instead he offered food and assistance to marchers. This was enough for the archbishop to send him away from his mission to another part of the country.

▼ Baptist churches could become targets of attack. The 16th Street Baptist Church in Birmingham, Alabama, was the site of a racist bombing in 1963 in which four young girls died. It is now a national landmark in commemoration of the victims and of the civil rights struggle.

ORGANIZATIONS

Many marchers joined the protest because they were members of civil rights organizations. The main ones in the late 1950s through the 1960s were the SCLC and the Student Nonviolent Coordinating Committee (SNCC). Julian Bond was a founding member of the SNCC. In an interview in 2010, he recalled why he joined their protests in the most segregated parts of the United States, saying: "Because we were young…we dared to take risks that our elders didn't take. They told us that in Mississippi, segregation could only be attacked from the outside, and we went right to the heart of the beast and attacked it there and beat it there."

THE FUTURE...

The future means redoubled efforts to continue . . .
- —introducing educated and determined young workers into hard core areas;
- —maintaining a college contact that leads to militant action in cities and provides new recruits for full time work.

The future means . . .
- —expanding our pilot voter registration projects in cities to provide workers in surrounding counties.
- —finding more funds to support students willing to work at subsistence wages and share the life of the Southern rural Negro while trying to convince him of his rights.
- —providing more and better workshops and conferences on the meaning and techniques of nonviolent community action and political involvement.

Change will be slow, but change must take place. SNCC will need *three times our current staff* to do the job we have only begun. We will also need *three times our current budget.*

The future means your support . . .
- —in contributions and in stimulating your local community to break down every form of racial discrimination now.
- —in letting us know how we can help you and how you can help us.

DANVILLE, VA.

▲ This SNCC brochure states the aims of the organization.

HISTORY DETECTIVES:
NAVIGATING SOURCES

In your local library, you may find several books that mention civil rights. Some will be more useful than others. Navigate books using the contents or index, and locate relevant information for your research quickly by skimming the headings and looking at the pictures.

On the Internet, you may find millions of sources. One easy way to decide which ones to look at are the ends of web site addresses. Those produced by governments end in .gov, and educational organizations end in .edu. These may be less biased than commercial sites ending in .com.

WATCHING EYE

The U.S. government was concerned that civil rights protestors might encourage unrest and violence. It kept an eye on marchers using its intelligence agency, the **Federal Bureau of Investigation (FBI)**. Some FBI agents secretly joined civil rights organizations and marches. Others paid or threatened marchers to pass on information.

In 2012, researcher Dr. Christopher Phelps was looking at documents from during the civil rights march years on the FBI web site. He discovered in a letter that an unnamed man "currently employed by the NAACP as a labor relations official" had been "contacted on several occasions by New York Agents and has been cooperative." Through research, he discovered that the NAACP official was named Herbert Hill. Hill had helped the FBI locate political radicals, who they then intimidated or arrested. As Phelps says: "It is [ironic] that an official dedicated to civil rights…could simultaneously provide assistance in naming names that would [reduce] political and civil liberties."

WHERE DID PEOPLE MARCH?

On May 2, 1963, in Birmingham, Alabama, a big civil rights march was about to begin. Police had assembled around a park by the 16th Street Baptist Church. Thousands of black people looked on. Inside the church, there were 2,000 protestors. Len Holt was a reporter who witnessed what happened next. He wrote:

"Freedom! Freedom!" A roar arose from the church. The cops almost as one, faced the church. Some unleashed clubs from their belts. The faces of those I could see had turned crimson… Before I could get back to the motel the demonstrations began; 60 demonstrators were on their way, marching two abreast, each with a sign bearing an integration slogan. Dick Gregory, the nightclub comedian, was leading the group. At a signal, 40 policemen converged, sticks in hand. Up drove yellow school buses…

"Do you have a permit to parade?" asked the police captain.

"No," replied Gregory.

"No what?" asked the captain in what seemed to be a reminder to Gregory that he had not used a "sir."

"No. No. A thousand times No," Gregory replied.

The captain said, "I hereby place you all under arrest for parading without a permit, disturbing the peace and violating the injunction of the Circuit Court of Jefferson County…"

And for the next two hours this scene was repeated over and over as group after group of students strutted out of the church to the cheers of the spectators, the freedom chants of those being carried away in buses and a continuous banging on the floors and sides of the buses.

THE RIGHT PLACE TO PROTEST

Civil rights marches happened in many places across the United States, from the capital, Washington, D.C., to places facing extreme segregation in the South (see the map on page 34). March organizers chose Birmingham, Alabama, in 1963 for several reasons:

- Its population contained a high percentage of black people, and one of its most popular church leaders, Fred Shuttlesworth, strongly supported the civil rights protest. Protests would have many supporters.
- It was the most segregated large city in the South and known as "Bombingham" because there had been so many firebombings of churches and homes of prominent black activists.
- Its public safety commissioner, Eugene "Bull" Connor, was known for ordering the rough treatment of civil rights protestors.

Organizers informed the Birmingham authorities to expect a march and invited the media to attend. They did not predict how extreme the response of Connor and his men would be on May 3. Photos and reports of nonviolent black protestors knocked down by high-pressure water from fire hoses and attacked by police dogs appeared in newspapers and on television worldwide. This angered the public and helped to raise awareness of and support for the civil rights movement.

◀ Marcher Walter Gadsden is attacked by police dogs in Birmingham, Alabama. The police were attempting to clear peaceful civil rights protestors from the streets.

MARCH TACTICS

Once they had chosen where to march, civil rights marchers used different tactics to try to make their protests count. For example, the Birmingham march was preceded by a month of other protests as part of the Birmingham Campaign, which gained little publicity. At the start of May, campaign organizers, including Fred Shuttlesworth, James Bevel, and Martin Luther King, Jr., decided a change in tactics was necessary. Bevel realized that fewer black adults were marching because they risked arrest and would then probably lose their jobs. Jobs with reasonable pay for black people were uncommon in segregated Birmingham. Bevel came up with the idea of encouraging schoolchildren to march instead, to increase numbers without risking jobs. These marches became known as the Children's Crusades. Waves of children marched from the church to different stores and other sites in Birmingham, which they occupied until they were moved or arrested. In total, 2,000 children were arrested.

Not everyone agreed with Bevel's controversial tactic, saying it put children in danger. Some teachers even tried to stop children from leaving school buildings on march days, although some kids escaped through classroom windows! Despite some people's reservations, the Children's Crusades created a lot of media attention and highlighted the striking contrast between nonviolent child protestors and armed adult police.

▼ Young black protestors huddle and protect each other from high-pressure water hoses directed by firefighters trying to break up the Birmingham march in May 1963.

Another tactic was to use King's high profile as a civil rights leader to gain more attention. King toured cities throughout the country before the Birmingham Campaign to raise money. Organizers anticipated that King would be arrested by Connor and his police, and they rapidly spread news of his arrest across the United States. They then did not pay the sum of money necessary to get King out of jail immediately. This ensured that there was more media coverage of his arrest and imprisonment for peaceful protest.

Think About This

Was using children a good idea?

Using children to front marches was widely criticized—and not only by people opposed to civil rights. Politician Robert F. Kennedy supported the protests but said, "School children participating in street demonstrations is a dangerous business. An injured, maimed, or dead child is a price that none of us can afford to pay." Do you think the pros of this tactic outweighed the cons?

WHO IN HISTORY

FRED SHUTTLESWORTH
1922–2011
BORN: Mount Meigs, Alabama

ROLE: Shuttlesworth helped found the SCLC and co-led the Children's Crusades in Birmingham. He was a truck driver and cement worker who became a powerful preacher and joined the NAACP. The NAACP was banned in Alabama in 1956, but Shuttlesworth set up a Christian human rights organization to help black people before getting involved in the SCLC. He was beaten and bombed many times as a result. He invited King to come to the city to help bring change.

Did You Know?

Shuttlesworth was unhurt after his opponents exploded dynamite outside his bedroom as he lay in bed!

REPORTING CIVIL RIGHTS MARCHES

"A...mother wept in the street Sunday morning in front of a Baptist Church in Birmingham. In her hand she held a shoe, one shoe, from the foot of her dead child. We hold that shoe with her...

Only we can trace the truth, Southerner—you and I. We broke those children's bodies....

We—who go on electing politicians who heat the kettles of hate...

We, who know better, created a climate for child-killing by those who don't."

This powerful piece written by Gene Patterson appeared in the *Atlanta Constitution* newspaper on September 16, 1963, after the bombing of a church in Birmingham in which four young girls died. This was just a few months after the Children's Crusades. Some reporters for southern city papers, such as Patterson, had great sympathy for civil rights protesters, but not all papers printed such pieces. This was partly to protect their offices and reporters from being targeted by the KKK. Many newspapers in the 1950s and 1960s gave sparse accounts of civil rights marches and violence, using only basic information sent out by local newspaper offices. However, the *New York Times* devoted lots of reporters, time, and money to the civil rights marches and regularly gave front-page space to the stories. This newspaper helped make civil rights a high-priority political issue for the U.S. government.

CAPTURING MARCHES

Photographers working for newspapers and magazines captured thousands of images of the civil rights marches. Some—such as those of hoses being fired at children in Birmingham, the face of a beaten protester, or marchers whose route is blocked by armed soldiers—have become iconic. This means they represent something more than just the events they are showing. The Birmingham marchers, for example, represent all innocent or powerless people targeted by troops or other people in a position of power. They also remind us of the imbalance in power faced and challenged by civil rights protestors. Iconic images helped make many viewers support the civil rights cause.

▲ Here you can see demonstrators in Birmingham, Alabama, shouting and jeering at the cameraman and the police. See below for how pictures can tell different stories.

HISTORY DETECTIVES:
INTERPRETING A PHOTO

A photo of an event in a newspaper is rarely objective. It is usually subjective because a photographer, or the publication that printed the image, made choices about what to show and what to leave out to support a story. Be careful when researching photos. For example, contrast the photo on page 27 of the boy calmly facing a dog attack with the one above. Both were taken at the same event in Birmingham. Either viewed alone might make us think very differently about the behavior and attitude of the demonstrators and the police.

IN WASHINGTON

Many groups have organized mass marches in Washington, D.C., because it is the seat of national government. The first civil rights event planned in the city was the 1941 March for Jobs. In 1963, the same organizers, A. Philip Randolph and Bayard Rustin, realized that it was again time for a big march on the capital. They knew that the massive publicity for recent events in Birmingham, Alabama, would guarantee high attendance and media interest. This was the March on Washington for Jobs and Freedom.

Rustin put together an organizing team. They raised money for the march by selling badges and collecting contributions from people and groups sympathetic to their cause. They organized celebrities to attend, such as actors Sidney Poitier and Marlon Brando, and entertainers Harry Belafonte and Sammy Davis, Jr. They made publicity posters and pamphlets and planned transportation for protestors traveling from as far afield as Alabama and Arkansas. See the official program for the 1963 march at www.ourdocuments.gov/doc.php?flash=true&doc=96.

▼ Several famous stars turned up to support the cause and attract more protestors at the Washington, D.C., march. They included (front, from left to right) actor Charlton Heston, writer James Baldwin, actor Marlon Brando, and singer Harry Belafonte.

LOCATION

Organizers wanted to march on Capitol Hill, but the government opposed this because it was close to the White House. They suggested assembling by the Washington Monument and not marching at all. Negotiations between the two sides resulted in a march from this assembly point to the nearby Lincoln Memorial. This monument was symbolic for black people because Abraham Lincoln was the president who had played a major role in the **emancipation** of slaves in the 19th century. But a large pool in front of the memorial meant there was not much space. Organizers had planned for 150,000 protestors, but estimated that nearly twice this number turned up.

MARCH ON WASHINGTON FOR JOBS AND FREEDOM
AUGUST 28, 1963

LINCOLN MEMORIAL PROGRAM

1. The National Anthem	Led by Marian Anderson.
2. Invocation	The Very Rev. Patrick O'Boyle, Archbishop of Washington.
3. Opening Remarks	A. Philip Randolph, Director March on Washington for Jobs and Freedom.
4. Remarks	Dr. Eugene Carson Blake, Stated Clerk, United Presbyterian Church of the U.S.A.; Vice Chairman, Commission on Race Relations of the National Council of Churches of Christ in America.
5. Tribute to Negro Women Fighters for Freedom Daisy Bates Diane Nash Bevel Mrs. Medgar Evers Mrs. Herbert Lee Rosa Parks Gloria Richardson	Mrs. Medgar Evers
6. Remarks	John Lewis, National Chairman, Student Nonviolent Coordinating Committee.
7. Remarks	Walter Reuther, President, United Automobile, Aerospace and Agricultural Implement Wokers of America, AFL-CIO; Chairman, Industrial Union Department, AFL-CIO.
8. Remarks	James Farmer, National Director, Congress of Racial Equality.
9. Selection	Eva Jessye Choir
10. Prayer	Rabbi Uri Miller, President Synagogue Council of America.
11. Remarks	Whitney M. Young, Jr., Executive Director, National Urban League.
12. Remarks	Mathew Ahmann, Executive Director, National Catholic Conference for Interracial Justice.
13. Remarks	Roy Wilkins, Executive Secretary, National Association for the Advancement of Colored People.
14. Selection	Miss Mahalia Jackson
15. Remarks	Rabbi Joachim Prinz, President American Jewish Congress.
16. Remarks	The Rev. Dr. Martin Luther King, Jr., President, Southern Christian Leadership Conference.
17. The Pledge	A. Philip Randolph
18. Benediction	Dr. Benjamin E. Mays, President, Morehouse College.

"WE SHALL OVERCOME"

▲ This primary source is the program of events for the famous march on Washington, D.C., at the Lincoln Memorial in 1963.

DIVIDED OPINIONS

Protestors present on the day could not agree about whether the Washington, D.C., event achieved its goals. SNCC executive Avon Rollins said: "I was awestruck by the multi-colored faces of the marchers... We all were joined together that day, equalized by our purpose for social and economic change in America. I felt that I was truly an eyewitness to history."

But some members of the SNCC had wanted to use the day for disruption in Washington, D.C., such as jamming telephone lines in government buildings and chaining themselves to the White House. SNCC organizer Julius Lester said: "The March was nothing but a giant therapy session that allowed Dr. King to [speak] about his dreams of a [black man] eating at the same table with some [southern white person], while most black folks just dreamed about eating."

MARCHING ORDERS

Organizers carefully controlled the march on Washington, D.C., in a variety of ways. They had a list of official demands to make to the government. These included making new laws guaranteeing all Americans decent housing, adequate and integrated education, the right to vote, and a fair minimum wage. To make sure the government heard the speeches, organizers invited every congressman and senator to the Lincoln Memorial at 12:00 on the day. Organizers insisted that marchers only carried banners with slogans that they provided. These represented the official demands of the march, to help onlookers understand why protestors were marching.

Many other practical details were planned, too. Marchers were asked to bring packed lunches, since many city center stores were closed on the day of the march. Spouts were attached to fire hydrants so marchers would have access to drinking water on or near the marching route. Organizers requested that every bus or train bringing marchers to Washington, D.C., had a "captain" or person responsible for the welfare and discipline of marchers. Over 2,000 volunteer marshals who were members of the SNCC or other groups were on hand to help direct marchers.

▼ These are the sights of some of the most famous civil rights marches and protests.

POLITICAL CHANGE

The march on Washington, D.C., and civil rights protests staged across the South spurred the U.S. government to make a change. President Kennedy was **assassinated** before his proposed changes to civil rights laws had been approved by the government. This took over a year, because southerners argued the bill would affect the rights of individuals and states in making their own laws. In 1964, President Lyndon B. Johnson finally pushed through the **Civil Rights Act**, banning segregation in public places and in employment on the grounds of race or religious beliefs. Jim Crow laws about segregation were overturned, and within a few years, most signs saying "Colored" or "White-Only" were removed across the South. However, unofficial segregation did persist, and the new focus of marches was to make it possible for more black people to vote, so that they could choose who represented them in government.

CIVIL RIGHTS MARCHES

Where	When	Number marching	How far they marched
Albany Movement: Albany, Georgia	1961	2,000	1 mile (1.6 kilometers)
Birmingham Campaign: Birmingham, Alabama	May 1963	6,000	1 mile (1.6 kilometers)
March on Washington for Jobs and Freedom: Washington, D.C.	August 1963	200,000	1 mile (1.6 kilometers)
March for Voting Rights: Selma–Montgomery, Alabama	1965	600–25,000	50 miles (80 kilometers)
March against Fear: Memphis, Tennessee, to Jackson, Mississippi	1966	1 initially, growing to 15,000	220 miles (354 kilometers)
Poor People's March: Washington, D.C.	1968	3,000	1 mile (1.6 kilometers)

WHAT HAPPENED TO PEOPLE ON THE MARCHES?

On the morning of March 7, 1965, a group of marchers left the Brown Chapel African Methodist Episcopal Church in Selma, Alabama. Their aim was to stage a march from Selma to Montgomery, the Alabama state capital. They wanted to protest primarily about black people not being able to vote in the state, but also about the death of a marcher named Jimmie Lee Jackson in the previous month. Many were dressed in their Sunday-best clothes and planned to walk only part of the 50-mile (80-kilometer) route to show their support. But the SCLC marchers and organizers knew that the state police, led by Sheriff Jim Clark, would try to stop them. One of the marchers was Amelia Boynton. In an interview in the 1980s, she described what she saw on the outskirts of the town:

> Just before we got to the light across the [Edmund Pettus] bridge, we saw that the road was blocked. I didn't think anything was going to happen, but as we approached, it was announced, "Don't go any farther." And when Hosea Williams said, "May I say something?" Clark said, "No, you may not say anything. Charge on them, men!" And they started beating us. They had horses. And I saw them when they were beating people down, and I just stood. Then one guy hit me with…a nightstick just back of the head and down toward the shoulder. And I still stood up there. Then the second [strike] was at the base of the neck. And I fell…

BLOODY SUNDAY

The day of this first Selma to Montgomery march came to be called **Bloody Sunday**. Around 200 police and state troopers, plus an armed group put together by the sheriff, charged the 600 marchers on horses, hitting them with clubs, plastic tubing wrapped in barbed wire, and whips. The officers wore gas masks and exploded **tear gas** bombs in the crowd. Tear gas makes people choke and their eyes water uncontrollably. The officers beat the protestors while they were struggling with the effects of the gas. They even chased, whipped, and hit injured protestors trying to retreat to the church. Injuries included deep cuts, broken teeth, fractured ribs, and concussions. This is how the *New York Times* reported on Bloody Sunday: www.nytimes.com/packages/html/books/mlk-rout.pdf.

The violence against marchers horrified the nation. When the marchers regrouped two days later, supporters arriving in Selma swelled their numbers. They marched again, but this time the event was more symbolic. They went to the bridge, knelt, and prayed for the injured in view of the waiting police, state troopers, and onlookers, including reporters. The second march is often called Turnaround Tuesday. Just under two weeks later, an even larger group marched. But on this third and final march, the marchers had government protection from racist violence, including armed members of the National Guard, and made it to Montgomery.

▼ The three Selma to Montgomery marches went through several Alabama counties where black people were denied the right to vote.

ABUSE

*People used to tickle me, talking about how brave I was...
marching...because I was so scared. All the time. It was like
wall-to-wall terrified. I can remember sitting in class, many times,
before demonstrations, and I knew, like, we were going to have a
demonstration that afternoon. And the palms of hands would be so
sweaty, and I would be so tense and tight inside. I was really afraid.*

This quote by Diane Nash shows how she knew that protesting for civil
rights was dangerous. Protestors could expect abuse, especially in places
in the South where there were many people fiercely against an end to
segregation, in addition to aggressive troops and officers upholding local
laws. The abuse could be verbal, such as name-calling. Physical violence
ranged from slapping and shoving to beatings with anything from sticks
to electric cattle prods. In Birmingham, Alabama, the water from hoses
directed at marchers was powerful enough to rip the bark from trees. It
knocked protestors down and caused bruising or even internal bleeding.

▼ Martin Luther King, Jr. (fifth from the right) leads civil rights activists
from Selma to Montgomery.

HISTORY DETECTIVES: TIMELINES

During research into a historical topic, you may end up with lots of information. Organize this information into a timeline so that it is easier to understand. Timelines help establish the order of events in a period of history. They can use different scales—for example, by month and year or by day during one month.

Timeline of the Selma marches

March 7: Bloody Sunday: First and most violent march at Selma. Around 50 of the 600 marchers were injured by troops and police officers soon after setting off.

March 9: Turnaround Tuesday: 2,000 marchers stopped before the Pettus Bridge to pray for the victims before returning to Selma.

March 21: Selma to Montgomery: Thousands marched over 50 miles (80 kilometers) to Montgomery, escorted and protected by troops sent in by President Johnson.

TESTING NONVIOLENCE

Civil rights organizations told protestors not to hit back at aggressive segregationists, but it was not always easy to remain nonviolent. On Bloody Sunday, at least one police officer was injured by retreating protestors throwing bricks. A few months earlier, Annie Lee Cooper had been waiting to register as a voter when Sheriff Clark poked her in the neck with his club, twisted her arm, and tried to force her home. She punched Clark, almost knocking him over, and his response was to hit her on the head hard with his club and throw her into jail. Some people praised her for taking a beating on their behalf. But civil rights leader James Bevel said **retaliation** did not help the cause because: "Then [the press] don't talk about the registration. We want the world to know they ain't registering nobody!"

You can see reports of people injured by police on the Birmingham march in 1963 on www.archives.state.al.us/teacher/rights/lesson3/doc6.html.

ANTICIPATING REACTIONS

Organizers told marchers what to expect during their protests. They expected to be arrested, since they would be breaking many laws by marching. For example, Selma courts made a ruling in 1964 that if five or more people were found congregating on the streets discussing the right to vote, they would be arrested. King ordered the return to Selma on Turnaround Tuesday because he did not want to anger a white judge sympathetic to the civil rights cause who was in the process of overturning this law. Marchers were also trained in how to protect themselves if they were attacked. Diane Nash recalls training classes when she was a student:

> We would practice things such as how to protect your head from a beating, how to protect each other, if one person was taking a severe beating, we would practice other people putting their bodies in between that person and the violence. So that the violence could be more distributed and hopefully no one would get seriously injured. We would practice not striking back, if someone struck us.

◀ "[Sheriff] Jim Clark couldn't see from the other movements that what he was doing to us was not only playing into our hands but going to bring the nation down on him," said Hosea Williams, national director of voter registration and political education for the SCLC, in 1965.

PREVENTED FROM VOTING

In 1870, the 15th Amendment to the Constitution became law, saying that no citizen should be denied the right to vote based on race or color. Yet in the early 1960s, most black people were still denied this right in the South. This was because state governments used a range of restrictions on who could vote: people could vote only if they passed tests proving their knowledge, if their grandfather had voted in the past before 1867, if they owned property, or if they could pay a poll tax. These restrictions excluded most black people, who were usually poor, lacked education, and whose grandparents had often been in slavery. Also, the major political party in the South, the Democratic Party, only allowed white members. The restrictions meant that of those eligible to vote in the South, very few were officially registered to do so. The table shows **voter registration** in three counties of Alabama in 1964, before the Selma–Montgomery marches:

	Lowndes Co.	Dallas Co.	Perry Co.
Percentage of population that was black and over 21	70	51	60
Percentage of registered black voters	0	2	5

The successful Selma march culminated in a final rally of some 25,000 people by the steps of the capitol building in central Montgomery. King gave a stirring speech, saying:

They told us we wouldn't get here. And there were those who said that we would get here only over their dead bodies but all the world today knows that we are here and we are standing before the forces of power in the state of Alabama saying, "We ain't goin' let nobody turn us around."

He and other march leaders took a petition demanding changes to voting laws to the offices of Alabama governor George Wallace, but he refused to meet them. Nevertheless, it was clear that the end to voting segregation in the state was near.

GOING FURTHER

Some people were killed for taking part in civil rights protests. Murders were most numerous in the South, notably Mississippi, and many were a result of efforts by people to increase the number of black people registered to vote. For example, white racists murdered Reverend George Lee when he refused to take his name off a list of registered voters, and Herbert Lee was killed for attending classes about voter education.

▼ Two Alabama state troopers stand near the car in which Viola Liuzzo (see page 43) was murdered by members of the Ku Klux Klan.

Many protestors and their families also faced long-lasting retaliation from people opposing equal rights. For example, the principals of Birmingham schools were told to expel Children's Crusaders in 1963, and in 1964, Mississippi state authorities stopped food relief for poor people who wanted to register as voters, so families did not have enough to eat. Many protestors' businesses were destroyed or harmed—for example, by firebombing, by being refused loans at banks, or by having deliveries of goods stopped.

MARCH DEATHS IN ALABAMA

The Selma marches were framed by several tragic deaths of protestors at the hands of those who violently opposed segregation.

Jimmie Lee Jackson: On the night of February 17, 1965, a night march from Selma to nearby Marion ended in tragedy. Jimmie Lee Jackson was shot and killed by police as he tried to protect his mother, whom the police were beating. This created outrage in the black community, but it was not reported widely in the national media. Organizer Jim Bevel said, "It would be fitting to take Jimmie Lee's body and march it all the way to the state capitol in Montgomery." This was what prompted the first Selma to Montgomery march.

James Reeb: Reeb was a white minister from Boston who had come to Selma to march. On the night of Turnaround Tuesday, Reeb and two black companions strayed into an area of town where local black people would normally never go. Reeb was hit with a club by a white man and refused treatment at the local Selma hospital. He died on the way to a Birmingham hospital. This death caused national outrage. Stokely Carmichael of the SNCC said: "What you want is the nation to be upset when anybody is killed...but it almost [seems that] for this to be recognized, a white person must be killed."

Viola Liuzzo: Liuzzo took part in the successful third march on Montgomery. Afterward, she offered to take marchers to Montgomery airport in a car with her black friend. Four KKK members spotted Viola, who was white, with her friend. They drove alongside the car and shot Liuzzo dead. This was a reminder to the marchers that despite their success in the third march, there was still a long battle to be fought.

PROTEST MUSIC

One cannot describe the…emotion this one song evokes across the Southland. I have heard it sung in great mass meetings with a thousand voices singing as one… I've heard the students singing it as they were being dragged away to jail. It generates power that is indescribable.

In this quotation, Wyatt T. Walker, an SCLC leader, was talking about the song "We Shall Overcome," the unofficial anthem of the civil rights movement. Many protestors, especially those in the SCLC, were used to singing traditional hymns and **gospel** songs in black churches. They also sang a lot while marching, often in time with the walking pace. Some songs even had words about marching:

Onward, Christian soldiers
Marching as to war…

But marchers sang many different types of music, not just church music. These included popular soul or blues songs of the day such as "I Wish I Knew (How It Would Feel to Be Free)" by Nina Simone, "This Little Light of Mine" by Sam Cooke, and Curtis Mayfield's "Keep on Pushing," written after the Washington, D.C., march.

Civil rights leaders knew that singing together was important for marchers because it created unity in the cause. This is why they often organized concerts at meetings and rallies featuring professional musicians. Some of these performers grew more famous and spread civil rights songs to a much wider audience as a result. These included the gospel singer Mahalia Jackson, who sang before many of King's speeches. Jackson was an SCLC organizer who described what was special about her singing:

When there is no gap between what you say and who you are, what you say and what you believe—when you can express that in song, it is all the more powerful.

You can listen to some recordings of civil rights songs from the 1960s at www.teachersdomain.org/asset/iml04_vid_music.

▲ Nina Simone wrote the song "Mississippi Goddam" after feeling great anger about the murder of Medgar Evers and the Birmingham church bombing in 1963. The song was banned by several radio stations, but it was popular among civil rights activists.

HIDDEN MESSAGES

In 2005, Robert Darden, a music historian, started the Black Gospel Music Restoration Project. He found old **singles** from the civil rights protest years, converted the music to digital files, and cataloged them into an archive to preserve the work. Darden discovered that the A-sides of records usually had a Christian message, but the B-sides called for support for the civil rights movement. For example, The Friendly Four's "Pray Before the Storm Comes" had a B-side called "Where Is Freedom?," which has lyrics about marches, demonstrations in Birmingham, integration, violence, and snapping police dogs. Darden says, "Few radio stations, which mainly were white-owned, were…playing gospel music at all, so [the records] were not widely circulated. And what was on the B-side mostly was being listened to in the black community. It was a kind of private message."

VOTING RIGHTS

What happened on Bloody Sunday, coupled with the restraint shown by marchers on Turnaround Tuesday, encouraged President Johnson to pressure Congress into changing voting rights laws. He knew that if he did not act fast, then more people would be hurt. This could affect government popularity, which was already low because he had decided to call up citizens to fight in the **Vietnam War**. On August 6, with King and other civil rights leaders watching, Johnson signed the **Voting Rights Act of 1965**. This prohibited stopping any U.S. citizen from voting based on the person's race or color and abolished voting restrictions. Within months, black voter registration rose dramatically in the South. But these were the last big civil rights protests that mobilized large numbers of both black and white people in a common cause.

WHO IN HISTORY

LYNDON B. JOHNSON
1908–1973

BORN: Stonewall, Texas

ROLE: As president, Johnson pushed through both the Civil Rights Act of 1964 (and its amendment in 1968) and the Voting Rights Act of 1965. His pro-civil rights beliefs lost him the support of many people in the Democratic Party in southern states. He also led the United States into a large-scale war in Vietnam.

Did You Know?

As a young man, Johnson was a teacher in a segregated Mexican school in Texas.

RIOT AND LAST MARCH

In 1965, there was a major race riot in Watts, Los Angeles, sparked by the arrest of a black driver by a white police officer. Cars were burned and stores smashed and looted, mostly by black residents. Over 10,000 members of the National Guard were called in to restore order; 34 people were killed and thousands were arrested. King and many other civil rights leaders knew that such violence would reduce nationwide approval for civil rights protests. They turned their attention toward the root causes of unrest and riots in northern cities. These included poor housing and low-paying jobs. King helped organize a Poor People's Campaign, including a march on Washington, D.C., to demand, for example, a higher minimum wage. However, before the march took place, King was assassinated. You can read press reports about the Poor People's Campaign at www.pbs.org/wgbh/amex/eyesontheprize/story/15_poor.html.

The last significant civil rights march took place after King's death and was led by his widow, Coretta Scott King, but it was not a success. Marchers were to walk to central Washington, D.C., and stay in a settlement of plywood shacks called Resurrection City on parkland. But the campaign soon started to run out of funds for building. New SCLC leader Ralph Abernathy negotiated with police to not arrest too many demonstrators because of low turnout. After six weeks, the campaign's permit for staying on the park ran out, and the National Guard closed Resurrection City.

▼ President Johnson (right) meets Martin Luther King, Jr., in the White House in 1966. The president was a champion of the civil rights movement.

WHAT HAPPENED TO MARCHERS AFTERWARD?

This is the 27th time I have been arrested, and I ain't going to jail no more!... We want black power! That's right... We don't have to be ashamed of it... We've begged the federal government—that's all we've been doing, begging and begging. It's time we stand up and take over. Every courthouse in Mississippi ought to be burned down tomorrow to get rid of the dirt and the mess. From now on, when they ask you what you want, you know what to tell 'em. What do you want? Black power.

Stokely Carmichael

BLACK POWER

These are the words of Stokely Carmichael of the SNCC after being arrested during the 1966 March against Fear in Mississippi. This march had been organized as a lone march by James Meredith, but Carmichael and Martin Luther King, Jr., took over after Meredith was shot and injured.

THE BLACK PANTHER PARTY

The Black Panther Party was founded in California by students Huey Newton and Bobby Seale. The group had a list of 10 goals for the party, including giving every black person the land and property originally promised to their slave ancestors at the time of emancipation and ending police brutality. View the group's Ten Point Platform at depts.washington.edu/civilr/display.cgi?image=bpp/docs/BPP4-8.jpg. Black Panther Party members wore black leather jackets and berets and carried guns, which were often not loaded. The government described the group as "government enemy number one," yet the party helped many poor black communities in California and Chicago—for example, by giving out food and providing health care.

Carmichael joined the **Black Panther Party** soon after, and his phrase "black power" became famous in the late 1960s. It symbolized a change of attitude among some civil rights protestors.

Many black people were deeply frustrated that the United States was spending billions of dollars overseas on the Vietnam War when many Americans were living in poverty. People like Carmichael said that nonviolence was not working and that only the threat of violence could bring about social change in the United States. They also said that black people should be more independent of white people. The SCLC accused Carmichael of being a black racist. Infighting within the Black Panther Party and other groups about leadership and tactics, as well as the blocking of their activities by the FBI, ended the black power movement in the 1970s.

INTO GOVERNMENT

Other civil rights protesters used the political skills they had developed through taking part in and organizing marches to eventually become representatives in government. Jesse Jackson had been a close colleague of King's, and he went on to become a senior Democratic Party member. In 1986, John Lewis of the SNCC was elected to represent Georgia in the U.S. House of Representatives.

▲ Controversially, sprinter Tommie Smith gave the black power salute during the 200-meters medal ceremony at the 1968 Olympic Games in Mexico.

OTHER CAUSES

Some marchers shifted their focus from the civil rights of black people to those of other groups. March organizer and protestor Bayard Rustin went on to defend Jewish people persecuted in the Soviet Union and campaigned for **gay rights** in the United States. Rustin was forced to leave the SCLC because he was gay. In 1986, he said: "The [test] of where one is on human rights questions is no longer the black community, it's the gay community...the community which is most easily mistreated."

Audrey Hendricks was one of the Children's Crusaders in Birmingham, Alabama, who was arrested for two weeks when she was eight years old. Hendricks went on to college in Texas and worked with children in residential centers who had emotional problems. The singer Harry Belafonte used his fame to encourage the support of stars for civil rights marches. He has since used this influence to support campaigns against HIV/AIDS, inequalities in world education, and world hunger. Belafonte is a goodwill ambassador for the global UNICEF organization that helps the children of the world. In 2012, he said: "Civil rights is a not a movement; it's a way of life. I'm saddened when I hear people say that the movement is over, for nothing could be further from the truth."

HISTORY DETECTIVES:
BIOGRAPHIES AND AUTOBIOGRAPHIES

Many civil rights marchers wrote autobiographies or feature in biographies. You can see a selection at multcolib.org/homework-center/civil-rights-biographies. Biographies can be fascinating summaries of lives and use primary sources within them. Autobiographies are primary sources.

Both types of source can have historical inaccuracies. An author may create an autobiography that presents him or her in a favorable way at the expense of getting all the facts right. Whatever sources you use for research, it is a good idea to double check key dates and facts against at least one other source.

H: This is an interview with Audrey Faye Hendricks for the Birmingham Civil Rights Institute's Oral History Project. I am Dr. Horace Huntley. We are at Miles College. Today is June 1, 1995.

Welcome, Ms. Hendricks.

HE: Thank you.

H: Thank for taking time out of your schedule to come and sit with us today. I would just want to start by asking you some general kinds of questions about your family. Where are your parents from? Are they originally from Birmingham?

HE: My mother is from Birmingham -- is a native Birminghamian. My father is a native of Boligee, Alabama which is in Greene County.

H: I see. Where were you born?

HE: I was born in Birmingham.

H: How many brothers and sisters are there?

HE: There are two of us. I am the oldest of two girls.

H: Tell me just a bit about the education of your parents. How much schooling did they have.

HE: My mother finished Booker T. Washington Business College and my father did not complete elementary school, being in a rural township.

H: What were their occupations?

HE: My father was a laborer. He worked for Jim Dandy at the time and my mother worked for Alexander and Company with a black insurance company at that time doing clerical kinds of things.

H: Tell me about your education. Where did you start school? Did you start at Center Street?

HE: I started at Center Street. I went there for four years. And after the four years I went to

▲ This primary source is the transcript of an interview with Audrey Hendricks conducted by Horace Huntley on June 1, 1995.

WHAT DIFFERENCE DID I MAKE?

Other protesters questioned whether the marches had been as successful as they could have been. Prathia Hall was present on Bloody Sunday, and what she saw made her lose some faith in nonviolent protest. She later said, "We might have had even greater power if we had somehow found a way to allow space for the expression of righteous anger."

WHY WERE THE MARCHES SIGNIFICANT?

In 2008, the American people elected their first black president, Barack Obama. This is a stunning example of the significance of the civil rights marches in transforming politics. The marches helped bring in the Voting Rights Act, which gradually increased the number of black representatives in government. The first senior black U.S. diplomats included Colin Powell and Condoleeza Rice, who were secretaries of state under President George W. Bush. In his inaugural address of 2013, Obama said:

> We, the people, declare today that the most evident of truths—that all of us are created equal—is the star that guides us still; just as it guided our forebears through…Selma…; just as it guided all those men and women, sung and unsung, who [marched]…to hear [Martin Luther King, Jr.] proclaim that our individual freedom is [tightly] bound to the freedom of every soul on Earth.

The success of nonviolent marches in improving civil rights inspired other groups to use it as a tactic to increase awareness of their cause. In 1970, for example, the first Gay Pride marches took place in U.S. cities, including Los Angeles. They were meant to raise awareness of the civil rights difficulties faced by gay and lesbian people. Today, Gay Pride marches happen worldwide.

Think About This

Equality

Do you think there is real equality for everyone? Consider how physical ability, age, sex, wealth, religion, and nationality affect people's rights. Which lead to the best equal rights, and which the worst? Does this vary depending on where in the world people live?

EVENTUAL JUSTICE

Doug Jones was nine when he heard that the KKK had firebombed the 16th Street Baptist Church on September 15, 1963, and killed four girls (see page 23). The FBI suspected four men of carrying out the bombing, but witnesses were reluctant to talk because they feared retaliation.

Jones studied law in college, and in 1977, he witnessed the trial and conviction of one of the suspects, Robert Chambliss. But there was insufficient evidence to convict the other suspects because some evidence was in secret FBI files. Twenty years later, the FBI material was **declassified**, and Jones's team reopened the case. They researched notes, photographs, and films from the 1960s and reinterviewed people to help link the suspects with the bombing. In a film they spotted one suspect, Bobby Cherry, in a mob beating up Reverend Fred Shuttlesworth, who was pastor of the church. In an FBI secret recording, they heard Thomas Blanton describing how he would make a bomb. In 2001, Blanton was sent to prison for life. A year later, so was Cherry. Cases such as this illustrate how the marches were also significant because they helped create a fairer legal system.

▼ President Barack Obama and First Lady Michelle Obama walk in the inaugural parade after Obama was sworn in as the 44th president of the United States on January 20, 2009, in Washington, D.C.

BLACK IDENTITY

The civil rights marches had a big impact on how black people viewed themselves in the South. Julia Holmes grew up in Mississippi during the years of the civil rights movement and says:

> After the movement, I think that blacks just began to feel like they were worthy, that their self-esteem just went up sky high. And they felt that they didn't have to bow down to anybody, and that they felt that they were as good.

Holmes says that the marches and other events where black and white people protested alongside each other also helped mutual understanding:

> We wouldn't be as tolerant of each other as we are now because the movement forced the races to come together and work together. Before the movement, we had all these preconceived notions about how one race was, and usually these preconceived notions were wrong.

REMEMBERING THE MARCHES

The significance of the marches has been remembered and celebrated in many different ways. For example, in Montgomery, Alabama, the Southern Poverty Law Center and its educational center, the Civil Rights Memorial Center, commemorate the marches but also continue the work of protesters. The centers provide legal help and advice for the poor in the South and educate visitors about the events and significance of the civil rights movement.

Many artists have created works that help bring the civil rights protests to life. These include movies such as *The Long Walk Home* (1990) about the 1955 Montgomery bus boycott, and documentaries such as *Eyes on the Prize* (1987) by Henry Hampton. This tells the story of the civil rights movement in episodes using newsreels and images. Hampton focused on the bravery and tactics of black people in the struggle because:

> A hundred civil rights stories had been told, but it was always black people being saved by whites... [The stories] depicted black folks as poor, downtrodden and brutalized primitives... It was the strength of blacks that made the civil rights movement happen, with support from some whites.

▲ Today, people in the United States mark the anniversary of Bloody Sunday each year by holding a march over the Edmund Pettus Bridge outside Selma, Alabama. The route is part of the Selma to Montgomery National Historic Trail that commemorates the importance of this location in the civil rights movement.

HATE CRIMES

Sadly, a small number of white extremists continued the violence toward black people even after the civil rights marches. In 1981, two KKK members lynched and killed Michael Donald in Alabama. In 2011, a 49-year-old man, James Anderson, was beaten up and then killed by a gang of white teenagers in Jackson, Mississippi. Both Donald and Anderson were chosen because they were black.

Today, racist hate crimes are investigated thoroughly by police, tried more fairly than in the past, and those found guilty are punished. For example, one KKK man was executed for his part in Donald's death, and the local Klan he belonged to was bankrupted after being ordered to pay several million dollars in damages.

SEGREGATION TODAY

In 2012, researchers analyzed data about segregation in U.S. city neighborhoods over the previous century. They found that U.S. cities were at their most segregated in the 1960s, but today they are more integrated than at any time since 1910. There are virtually no all-white and fewer all-black neighborhoods than in the past. The civil rights movement reduced segregation, but many people in the United States still have different expectations in life depending on their race:

- Education: Test scores for children 9, 13, and 17 years old in math and reading are consistently higher for white children, although the gap between blacks and whites has decreased since the early 1970s.
- Jobs: The unemployment rate is two times higher for black people.
- Crime: Black people make up about 12 percent of the U.S. population, but they make up 40 percent of the prison population, and black people generally face longer sentences than white people do.

There are many reasons for these differences, including the fact that many urban blacks live in poorer neighborhoods, where there are social problems such as badly equipped schools with discipline problems.

▼ Young people paint murals for Martin Luther King, Jr., Day at a community center in the South Bronx, in New York. This area of the city has high rates of poverty and crime, poor schools, and housing—all problems that King and the civil rights movement tried to change.

NEW VOTING RESTRICTIONS

Many people in the United States are also concerned about changes that could affect how many black people vote. In some states, such as Florida, only those with photo ID can vote. Poorer black people are less likely to have the time, money, or transportation to obtain this new identification, so they might not vote. John Lewis, the SNCC founder and congressman, said in 2012:

> People are not being beaten and trampled by horses or tear gassed, people are not being shot and killed. The obstructions are not as obvious, but the effect…will damage the integrity of our political process for generations to come, if it is not corrected.

HISTORY DETECTIVES: FINISHING RESEARCH?

Imagine finding a lost diary by Martin Luther King, Jr., detailing how he felt about the marches or other civil rights leaders. New primary sources can emerge years after an event, either accidentally or through the work of researchers. They add to what we already know and help us get closer to an accurate story of human history. So, if you are starting research on a topic that has been studied and written about many times, remember that you might discover something new or interpret the facts in a new way, adding to people's understanding.

> The media and history seems to record it as Martin Luther King's movement, but if young people realized that it was people just like them, their age, that formulated goals and strategies, and actually developed the movement, that when they look around now, and see things that need to be changed…instead of saying, I wish we had a leader like Martin Luther King today, they would say, what can I do, what can my roommate and I do to effect that change.

Diane Nash

TIMELINE

1863	U.S. President Abraham Lincoln issues the Emancipation Proclamation. This frees "all slaves in areas still in rebellion."
1865	The 13th Amendment abolishes slavery
1896	The U.S. Supreme Court approves the "separate but equal" segregation doctrine
1909	The National Association for the Advancement of Colored People (NAACP) is formed
1925	The Ku Klux Klan marches on Washington, D.C., in its first national demonstration
1948	**July:** President Harry S. Truman issues an executive order outlawing segregation in the U.S. military
1954	**May:** The Supreme Court rules on Brown v. Board of Education, declaring that school segregation is unconstitutional
1955	**Aug.:** Emmett Till is lynched **Dec.:** Rosa Parks is jailed
1957	**Jan.:** Martin Luther King, Jr., and Charles Steele establish the Southern Christian Leadership Conference (SCLC) **Sept.:** The Little Rock Nine group of black students try to go to a segregated white school in Arkansas
1960	**Feb.:** Four black college students begin sit-ins at a Woolworth's lunch counter in Greensboro, North Carolina **April:** The SNCC is formed
1961	**May:** Freedom rides are met with violence **Nov.:** Albany Movement of sit-ins and protests begin against transportation facility segregation in Albany, Georgia

1962	**Oct.:** James Meredith is enrolled as the first black student at the University of Mississippi
1963	**Aug.:** March on Washington for Jobs and Freedom attracts 200,000 protestors, and King delivers his famous "I Have a Dream" speech **Sept.:** The KKK bomb the 16th Street Baptist Church in Birmingham, Alabama, leaving four young black girls dead **Nov.:** President John F. Kennedy is assassinated in Dallas, Texas; Lyndon B. Johnson is sworn in as the new president hours later
1964	**July:** The Civil Rights Act makes racial discrimination illegal **Aug.:** Three civil rights activists are murdered in Mississippi
1965	**Feb.:** Jimmie Lee Jackson is murdered in Alabama **March:** A march from Selma to Montgomery, Alabama, is organized to demand protection for voting rights; segregationist state forces attack and injure protestors on Bloody Sunday; Viola Liuzzo is murdered by the KKK **Aug.:** The Voting Rights Act makes it illegal to force would-be voters to pass tests in order to vote
1967	Thurgood Marshall becomes the first black Supreme Court justice
1968	**April:** King is assassinated in Memphis, Tennessee; President Johnson signs the Civil Rights Act of 1968 **May:** Poor People's Campaign in Washington, D.C., includes the last significant civil rights march, led by Coretta Scott King
2001–2002	Bobby Cherry and Thomas Blanton are convicted of the bombing of the 16th Street Baptist Church in 1963
2005	Edgar Ray Killen is convicted of the manslaughter of three civil rights activists murdered in Mississippi in 1964
2008	Barack Obama becomes the first black U.S. president

GLOSSARY

assassinated killed in a surprise attack

Baptist fifth-largest Christian community in the world, which takes its name from the Baptist practice of immersion in water

Black Panther Party political organization of the late 1960s that promoted increased power for black people, which could be gained by violent means

Bloody Sunday first Selma to Montgomery march, in 1965

boycott stop using, buying, or dealing with a person, organization, or country as a form of protest

Brown v. Board of Education law passed in 1954 making the segregation of schools illegal

civil rights rights of citizens to political and social freedom and equality

Civil Rights Act of 1964 law banning segregation in public places and in employment on the grounds of race or religious beliefs

civil rights movement campaign in the 1950s and 1960s to change laws so that black Americans had the same rights as others

congregation group of people assembled for religious worship

declassified reduction or removal by the government of restrictions on a classified document

desegregate open a place that was previously segregated to members of all races and ethnic groups

direct action use of strikes, demonstrations, or other public forms of protest rather than negotiation to achieve one's demands

discrimination treating a particular group in society unfairly—for example, because of their race or sex

emancipation freeing someone from the control of another

equality being equal in terms of status, rights, and opportunities

Federal Bureau of Investigation (FBI) U.S. government agency that deals with both criminal investigations and information-gathering

firebombing attack with bombs designed to start fires

freedom rides bus trips taken by black and white civil rights activists in the 1960s to challenge segregation on buses

gay rights equal rights for homosexuals

gospel style of black American evangelical singing, developed from religious songs sung in southern Baptist and Pentecostal churches

Jim Crow laws laws that kept black people from being treated as equals to whites

Ku Klux Klan (KKK) secret society that uses terrorism to promote white supremacy

lynching execution by a mob, usually by hanging

mission when people from a religious organization, especially a Christian one, travel the world to spread their faith, or the institution from which they work abroad

National Association for the Advancement of Colored People (NAACP) civil rights organization

National Guard reserve military force in the United States

persecution torment, harass, or abuse people, usually on the basis of their race, gender, or religion

retaliation action taken in return or in revenge for an injury or offense

segregation policy of separating people of different races, religions, or sexes and treating them in a different way

segregationist someone who believes people of different races should be kept apart

single short record with one song on each side

sit-in form of protest in which demonstrators occupy a place, refusing to leave until their demands are met

Southern Christian Leadership Conference (SCLC) civil rights organization led by religious leaders, including Martin Luther King, Jr.

Student Nonviolent Coordinating Committee (SNCC) civil rights organization made up mainly of young people

Supreme Court most important court in the United States that makes decisions affecting all the states

tear gas gas that causes severe irritation to the eyes, usually used to force crowds to disperse

Vietnam War war that lasted between 1954 and 1975 between the communist armies of North Vietnam, supported by China, and the armies of South Vietnam, who were supported by the United States

voter registration requirement of citizens to register with their local board of elections before being qualified to vote

Voting Rights Act of 1965 law making it illegal for a U.S. citizen to be prevented from voting based on the person's race or color and abolishing state restrictions on voter registration

FIND OUT MORE

BOOKS

Beals, Melba Pattillo. *Warriors Don't Cry*. New York: Simon Pulse, 2002.

Hynson, Colin. *The Civil Rights Movement* (Timelines). Mankato, Minn.: Arcturus, 2011.

Meany, John. *Has the Civil Rights Movement Been Successful?* (What Do You Think?). Chicago: Heinemann Library, 2009.

Moody, Anne. *Coming of Age in Mississippi*. New York: Dell, 1992.

WEB SITES

americanhistory.si.edu/brown/history/1-segregated/jim-crow.html
Visit this web site to read some of the Jim Crow laws.

www.thekingcenter.org
Learn about Martin Luther King, Jr., and how his work continues today.

www.loc.gov/teachers/classroommaterials/primarysourcesets/naacp/
This web site allows you to view many primary sources from the history of the NAACP.

memory.loc.gov/ammem/aaohtml/exhibit/aopart9.html
This web site includes a summary of key moments and people in the civil rights era, including links to primary sources.

www.pbs.org/wgbh/amex/eyesontheprize/index.html
The web site of the television series *Eyes on the Prize* is a fascinating, detailed account of the civil rights movement, including primary sources and reflections on an era by people who were there.

photos.state.gov/libraries/iran/19452/pdfs/free-at-last.pdf
See a full summary of the civil rights movement, from its beginnings with the end of slavery to the election of President Barack Obama in 2008.

PLACES TO VISIT

There are many museums and sites focusing on civil rights in the United States. Here are some places to visit:

Birmingham Civil Rights Institute
520 Sixteenth Street North
Birmingham, Alabama 35203
www.bcri.org

Civil Rights Memorial Center
400 Washington Avenue
Montgomery, Alabama 36104
www.splcenter.org/civil-rights-memorial

Martin Luther King, Jr., Memorial
West Potomac Park
1964 Independence Avenue, SW
Washington, D.C. 20001
www.nps.gov/mlkm/index.htm

National Museum of African American History and Culture
1400 Constitution Avenue, NW
Washington, D.C. 20004
nmaahc.si.edu

TOPICS TO RESEARCH

Emancipation:
In the 19th century, some slaves in the South helped bring about
emancipation by rebelling against slavery. Research the events leading up
to emancipation in 1863. How do these events reflect those leading up to
the Washington, D.C., march 100 years later?

Red Power:
In the 1960s, American Indians had the highest unemployment rates and
lowest average wages of the nation, in addition to suffering from poor
health and many negative stereotypes. Some American Indians started to
fight for improved civil rights, just as black Americans were doing. Research
the Declaration of Indian Purpose that led to the Red Power Movement and
American Indian Movement.

INDEX

Abernathy, Ralph 22, 47
Albany Movement 12–13, 35
Armstrong, James 18–19

Baptist Church 17, 22
Belafonte, Harry 32, 50
Bevel, James 28, 39, 43
Birmingham, Alabama 26, 27, 28, 30, 35, 38, 43, 45
Black Guard 17
Black Panther Party 48, 49
black politicians 49, 52
"black power" 17, 48–49
Bloody Sunday 36–37, 39, 46, 51, 55
boycotts 10, 14, 16
Brown v. Board of Education court case 8, 9

Carmichael, Stokely 43, 48, 49
celebrity supporters 32, 50
Children's Crusades 28, 29, 43, 50
church communities 17, 22–23
Civil Rights Act 35
Connor, Eugene "Bull" 27, 29

desegregation 13, 14, 20, 35
direct action 10, 14
discrimination 7, 8

education 7, 9, 10, 18, 56

Faubus, Orval 10, 11
FBI 25, 49, 53
films 19, 54
firebombing 11, 14, 16, 27, 30, 43, 53
freedom rides 14–15, 21
fundraising 29, 32

Gandhi, Mohandas 16
gay rights 50, 52

hate crimes 55
Heschel, Abraham Joshua 22

Jackson, Jesse 44, 49
Jackson, Jimmie Lee 36, 43
Jim Crow laws 7, 8, 9, 35
Johnson, Lyndon B. 35, 46, 47

Kennedy, John F. 4, 35
Kennedy, Robert F. 29
King, Jr., Martin Luther 5, 16, 17, 19, 22, 28, 29, 33, 38, 40, 41, 46, 47, 48
Ku Klux Klan (KKK) 4, 11, 17, 22, 30, 42, 43, 53, 55

Lewis, John 4, 21, 49, 57
Little Rock Nine 10, 11
Liuzzo, Viola 19, 42, 43
lynching 11, 20, 55

Malcolm X 17
March against Fear 35, 48
March on Washington for Jobs and Freedom 4–5, 32–35
media coverage 14, 29, 30
Montgomery Bus Boycott 10, 22, 54
mutual tolerance 54

National Association for the Advancement of Colored People (NAACP) 8, 25, 29
nonviolent protest 16, 17, 28, 39, 49, 51, 52

Parks, Rosa 10
Plessy v. Ferguson court case 7
police brutality 27, 28, 36–37, 39
Poor People's Campaign 35, 47

race riots 46–47
Reeb, James 43
research 9, 57
  biographies and autobiographies 50
  conflicting sources 13
  declassified material 53

inaccuracies 50
Internet research 17, 25
KWL chart 9
navigating sources 25
oral history 19
photographs 31
primary sources 11, 13, 15, 51
secondary sources 11
timelines 39, 58–59
Resurrection City 47
Rustin, Bayard 21, 32, 50

segregation 6, 7, 8, 9, 10, 11, 12, 14, 18, 20, 24, 35, 56
Selma–Montgomery marches 18, 22, 35, 36–41, 43
Shuttlesworth, Fred 22, 27, 28, 29, 53
Simone, Nina 44, 45
sit-ins 14
songs, protest 44–45
Southern Christian Leadership Conference (SCLC) 17, 24, 29, 36, 47, 49
student activism 20–21
Student Nonviolent Coordinating Committee (SNCC) 4, 24, 33

Thurgood, Marshall 8, 9
Till, Emmett 20
transportation 10, 12, 14–15
Turnaround Tuesday 37, 40, 46

violence 14, 27, 28, 36–37, 38, 39, 40, 42, 43
voting rights 35, 39, 41, 42, 46, 52, 57